It's Catching

Impetigo

Elizabeth Laskey

Heinemann Library
Chicago, Illinois

Designed by Patricia Stevenson
Printed and bound in the United States by Lake Book Manufacturing

07 06 05 04 03
10 9 8 7 6 5 4 3 2 1

Library of Congress Cataloging-in-Publication Data
Laskey, Elizabeth, 1961–
    Impetigo / Elizabeth Laskey.
       v. cm. — (It's catching)
    Includes bibliographical references and index.
    Contents: What is impetigo? — Healthy skin — What causes impetigo? —
    First signs — What happens next? — Don't scratch! —
    How impetigo spreads — Treatment — At home — Getting better —
    Avoiding impetigo — Staying healthy — Think about it.
    ISBN 1-4034-0274-4
    1. Impetigo—Juvenile literature. [1. Impetigo. 2. Diseases.]
    I. Title. II. Series.

RL283 .L37 2002
616.5'24—dc21

2001008562

Acknowledgments
The author and publishers are grateful to the following for permission to reproduce copyright material:
Cover photograph by Ken Greer/Visuals Unlimited
pp. 4, 10 Dr. P. Marazzi/SPL/Photo Researchers, Inc.; p. 5 Ariel Skelley/Corbis Stock Market; p. 6 Mitch Diamond/Index Stock Imagery/PictureQuest; p. 7 Jack Reznicki/Corbis Stock Market; p. 8 Oliver Meckes/Ottawa/Photo Researchers, Inc.; p. 9 Benelux Press/Index Stock Imagery/PictureQuest; p. 11 Ansary/Custom Medical Stock Photo, Inc.; p. 12 Biophoto Associates/Science Source/Photo Researchers, Inc.; p. 13 Myrleen Cate/PhotoEdit; p. 14 Jack Ballard/Visuals Unlimited; p. 15 Barts Medical Library/PhotoTake; p. 16 Bob Daemmrich/Stock Boston, Inc.; p. 17 Lawrence Migdale/Photo Researchers, Inc.; p. 18 Corbis; p. 19 Richard Gross/Corbis Stock Market; p. 20 Tony Freeman/PhotoEdit; p. 21 Photographers Library LTD/eStock Photography/PictureQuest; p. 22 David Young-Wolff/PhotoEdit/PictureQuest; p. 23 Ken Greer/Visuals Unlimited; p. 24 Charles D. Winters/Photo Researchers, Inc.; p. 25 The Image Bank/Getty Images; p. 26 Fotografia, Inc./Corbis; p. 27 Charles Gupton/Stock Boston, Inc./PictureQuest; p. 28 D. Yeske/Visuals Unlimited; p. 29 Norbert Schafer/Corbis Stock Market
Every effort has been made to contact copyright holders of any material reproduced in this book. Any omissions will be rectified in subsequent printings if notice is given to the publisher.

Some words are shown in bold, **like this.** You can find out what they mean by looking in the glossary.

What Is Impetigo?

Impetigo is a skin **infection.** The infection causes small **blisters** to form on your skin. The blisters break and a hard crust forms where the blisters were.

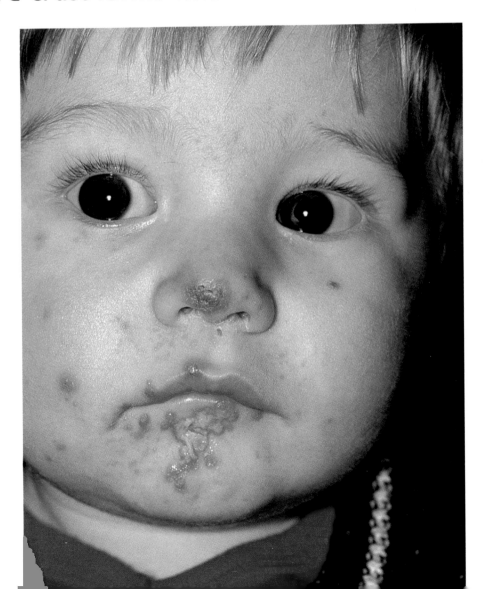

Contents

Impetigo is very **infectious.** This means that the infection can spread easily from person to person.

Healthy Skin

Skin covers the outside of your whole body. Your skin protects the inside of your body by keeping out dirt and **germs.** Germs are very tiny things that can make you sick if they get inside your body.

Many types of germs live on your skin.
They are so small you cannot see them.
Your skin keeps them from getting inside
your body.

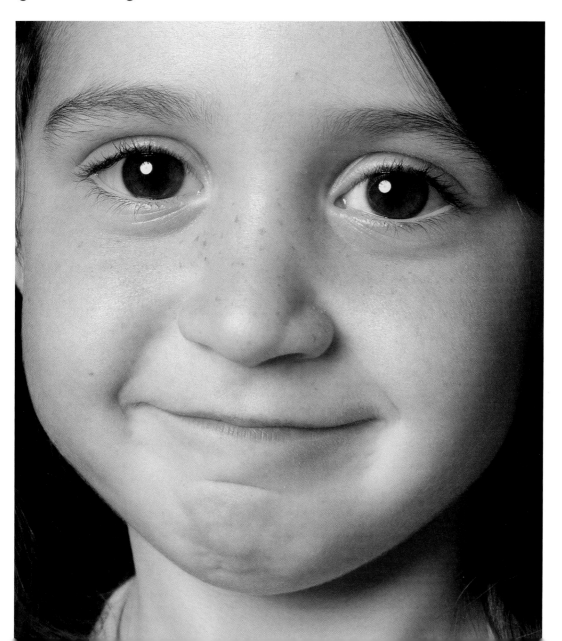

What Causes Impetigo?

Impetigo is caused by **bacteria.**
Bacteria are tiny living things. They are
so small you need a **microscope** to see
them. This is what impetigo bacteria look
like through a microscope.

Impetigo bacteria get into your body through a break in your skin such as a cut, scrape, or bug bite. When they get inside, they can give you impetigo.

First Signs

The first thing you see if you have impetigo are groups of tiny **blisters** on your skin. Often the blisters form around your nose and mouth.

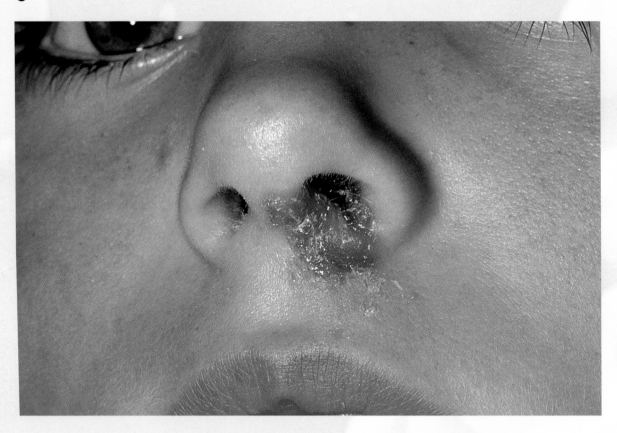

Sometimes the blisters are large. They can be the size of a dime or bigger.

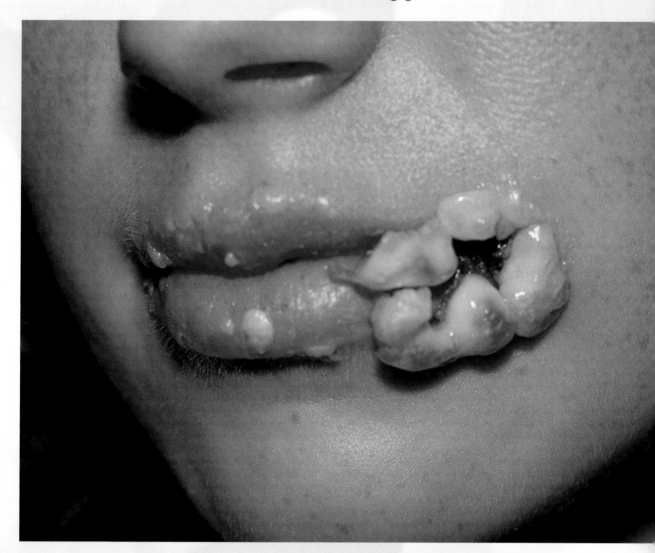

What Happens Next?

The **blisters** do not hurt, but they can itch a lot. The blisters break easily. When they break, liquid **oozes** out of the blisters and hardens into a yellow-orange crust, or **scab.**

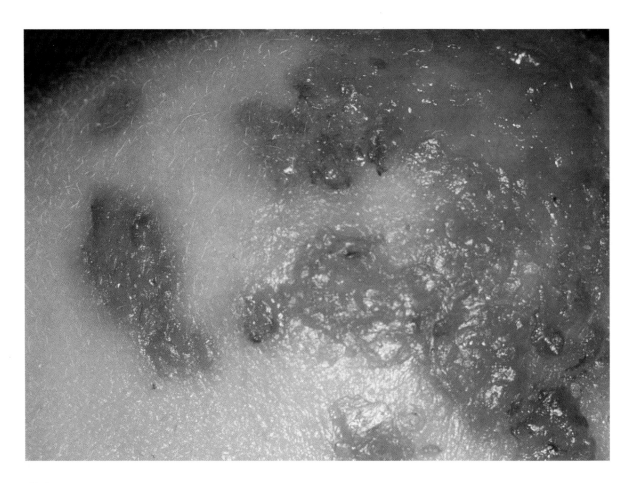

You will not feel sick if you have impetigo. But you shouldn't go to school or play with other children because impetigo spreads easily. You will need to go to a doctor.

Don't Scratch!

You will want to scratch the **blisters** because they are itchy. But the blisters and **scabs** are full of impetigo **bacteria.** If you scratch the blisters or scabs, the bacteria will get onto your fingers.

Then, if you touch another part of your body, impetigo blisters may form there. If you do scratch the **infected** skin by mistake, you should wash your hands right away.

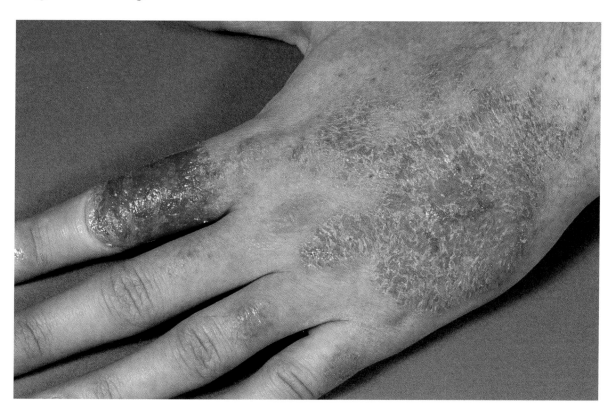

How Impetigo Spreads

Touching the impetigo **blisters** or **scabs** can spread impetigo. If you touch the **infected** skin and then touch another person, that person may get impetigo.

The impetigo **bacteria** may also be on your towels and sheets. If these things are not washed before another person uses them, that person can get impetigo.

Treatment

When you go to the doctor, he or she will give you an **antibiotic ointment** to put on the **infected** skin. Antibiotics are a kind of medicine that kills **bacteria.**

If the impetigo **blisters** are on many parts of your body, the doctor might give you antibiotic medicine to swallow. The antibiotic medicine will get rid of the impetigo bacteria inside your body.

At Home

When you have impetigo, it is important to keep your skin clean. An adult can help you wash the **infected** skin with soap and water.

If the doctor gives you **antibiotic ointment,** you should put it on the infected skin after it has been washed. A bandage will help keep the ointment from getting rubbed off.

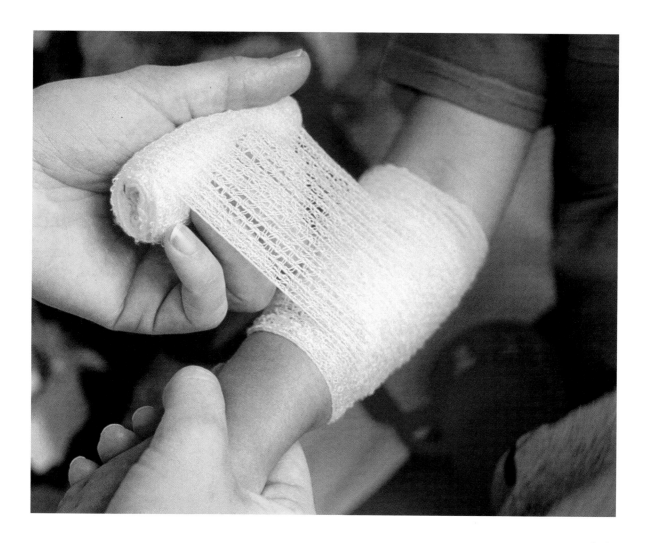

Getting Better

After you have used **antibiotics** for two days, you can go back to school and play with your friends again. After two days of taking antibiotics you won't be **infectious** anymore.

In about three days, the **blisters** and **scabs** will start to **heal** and go away. In about a week, they will be gone.

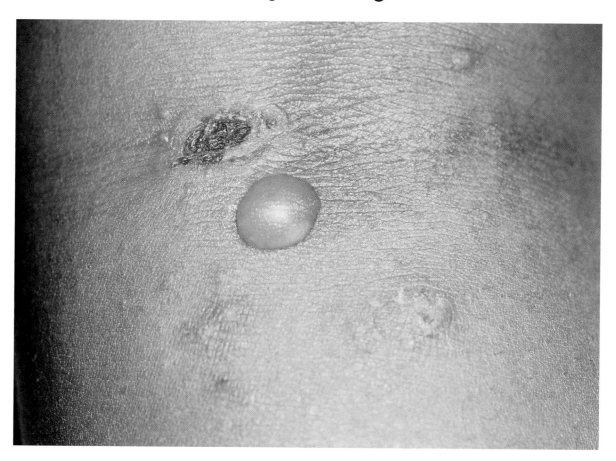

Avoiding Impetigo

Always be sure to clean a cut, scrape, or bug bite well. This will help keep it from getting **infected** with impetigo **bacteria.** Try not to scratch bug bites.

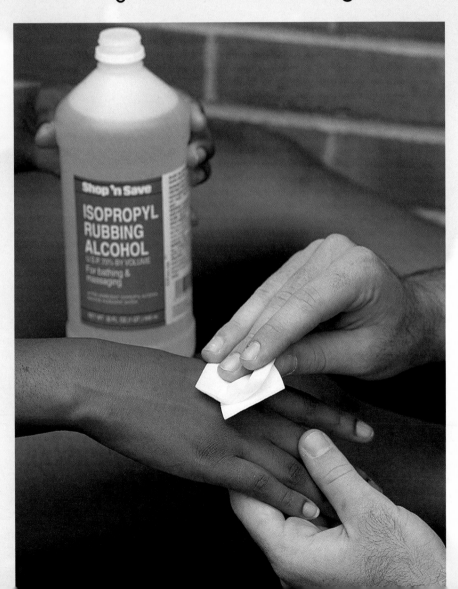

Do not use towels or washcloths that have been used by other people. This will also help keep you from getting impetigo.

Staying Healthy

Keeping clean is very important to keep from getting impetigo. Taking baths or showers often is a good idea.

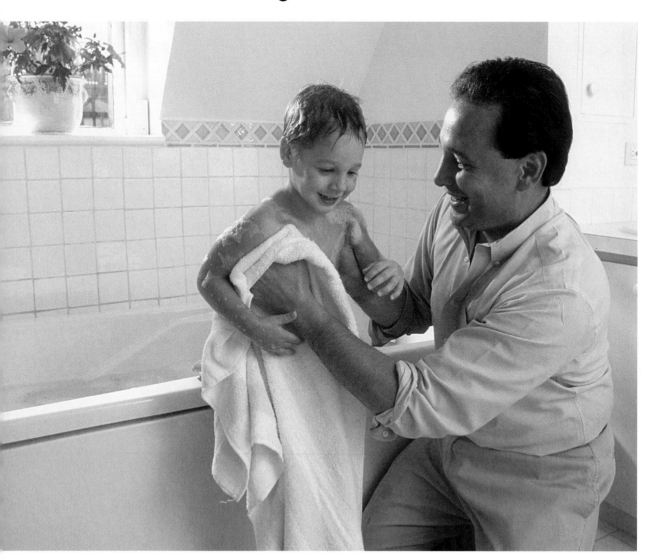

The best way to avoid getting sick is to eat well, exercise, and get enough sleep. This will help your body stay strong and healthy.

Think about It!

Amy has a lot of bug bites. Why shouldn't she scratch the bug bites?*

Casey has impetigo. Why can't Casey use the towels the rest of the family uses?*

*Read page 30 to find out.

Answers

Page 28

Amy should not scratch the bug bites because scratching could break the skin. Then, impetigo **bacteria** could get inside her body and cause her to get impetigo.

Page 29

Impetigo bacteria can get on the towels that a person who has impetigo uses. If Casey uses the family towels, other family members may get impetigo.

Stay Healthy and Safe!

1. Always tell an adult if you feel sick or think there is something wrong with you.

2. Never take any medicine or use any **ointment** unless it is given to you by an adult you trust.

3. Remember, the best way to stay healthy and safe is to eat good food, drink lots of water, keep clean, exercise, and get lots of sleep.

Glossary

antibiotic   medicine that kills bacteria

bacteria   tiny living things that can make you sick if they get in your body

blister   raised bump on the skin that is filled with liquid

germ   tiny thing that can make you sick if it gets in your body

heal   get well

infected   made sick or unhealthy by germs

infection   illness caused by germs that can spread from one person to another

infectious   can be passed from one person to another and can make you sick

microscope   machine that makes very small things look big enough to see

ointment   cream that has medicine in it and is rubbed onto the skin

ooze   leak out slowly

scab   hard crust that forms on the skin when liquid from a cut or blister dries

Index

More Books to Read

Rowan, Kate. *I Know How We Fight Germs.* Cambridge, Mass.: Candlewick
    Press, 1999.

Royston, Angela. *Clean and Healthy.* Chicago: Heinemann Library, 1999.

Saunders-Smith, Gail. *The Doctor's Office.* Minnetonka, Minn.: Capstone
    Press, 1998.